Tomorrow, We Will Live Here

RYAN VAN WINKLE is Reader in Residence at the Scottish
Poetry Library. He runs a monthly "Literary Cabaret" called The
Golden Hour and is an Editor at Forest Publications. He lives in
Edinburgh but was born and spent most of his life in America.
His work has appeared in *AGNI, The American Poetry Review, New
Writing Scotland, Northwords Now* and *The Oxford Poets* series.
He has won Salt's Crashaw Prize and been shortlisted for the
Bridport and Ver Poetry Prizes.

Tomorrow, We Will Live Here

by

RYAN VAN WINKLE

LONDON

PUBLISHED BY SALT PUBLISHING
Dutch House, 307–308 High Holborn, London WC1V 7LL United Kingdom

© Ryan Van Winkle, 2010

The right of Ryan Van Winkle to be identified as the
author of this work has been asserted by him in accordance
with Section 77 of the Copyright, Designs and Patents Act 1988.

Salt Publishing 2010

Printed in Great Britain by the MPG Books Group, Bodmin and King's Lynn

Typeset in Swift 9.5 / 13

ISBN 978 1 84471 789 7 paperback

1 3 5 7 9 8 6 4 2

for Helen

Contents

My 100-Year-Old Ghost	1
Thirteen	3
Cassella: The Pastor's Son	4
Hunter Boy & Girls at the Stream	5
I Was a Fat Boy	6
Tomorrow the Red Birds	7
Everybody Always Talking About Jesus	8
Night Nurse	11
Under Hotel Sheets	12
The Grave-tender	14
The Water is Cold	15
Gasoline	16
They Will Go On	18
Oregon Trail	19
The Apartment	20
The First Time I Touched Her	22
Our Door, After a Turbulence	24
Knots	25
Stain	26
Babel	27
The Slip (pt. 2)	28
Bluegrass	29
The Day He Went to War	31
Retrieving the Dead	32
Necessary Astronomy	33
The Flood	35
They Tore The Bridge Down a Year Later	36
Ode for a Rain from Death Row	40
I Got Out When It All Went Down	41

Open the Connections, She Says.   43
Last Night, I Should Have Driven Straight Home   45
Waiting for the Ocean   46
Also, it is Lambing Season   48
Unfinished Rooms   50
And Table, You are Made of Wood   56

Notes   59

Acknowledgements

Versions of poems in this collection have previously appeared in *FuseLit, The Golden Hour Book, The Golden Hour Book Vol. II, Gutter, New Leaf, New Writing Scotland: 26 & 28, Northwords Now, The Oxford Poets Anthology 2010, Tontine, Ver Poetry Prize Pamphlet 2007*, and *V: New International Writing from Edinburgh*. Grateful acknowledgment and thanks to these magazines and editors for their support.

I would like to thank Nick Holdstock for working with these poems before they were anything close to poems. Benjamin Morris was an essential editor whose careful eye was much appreciated throughout this process. Further gratitude is due to Shannon Allen, Krystelle Bamford, Dave Coates, Colin Fraser, Alan Gillis, Jane Griffiths, Aiko Harmon, Peggy Hughes, Robert Alan Jamieson, Russell Jones, Kapka Kassabova, Katherine Leyton and Jane McKie for making time to interrogate my work. Truly, my appreciation is huge. Special thanks to Mario Petrucci for opening up his box of experience. Massive thanks to all the volunteers at The Forest Arts Collective who continue to sustain me and much of Edinburgh. This book would probably not exist without the assistance, both financial and moral, of The Scottish Arts Council and The Scottish Poetry Library. I'd particularly like to thank Lilias Fraser and Robyn Marsack for their honest critiques and help in honing this work. Lee Smith, Chris Hamilton-Emery and all at Salt have been patient and wonderful to work with—thank you all for putting this together and making it happen. And lastly, a big kiss to all the fine friends, family members, writers, readers and listeners who have come to gigs, fed me and been supportive for a long time.

"Why leave when you can live in a place you can understand and that understands you?"

—BILL MCKIBBEN

My 100-Year-Old Ghost

sits up with me when the power cuts,
tells about the trout at Unkee's Lake,

the wood house burned on the hill.
He says he was intimate with every

leaf of grass. Wore one hat
for Griswold, another for his own field,

the possibilities of the century laid out;
an endless string of fishing pools. But

they never got ahead of my ghost—
he took them like cows, one at a time,

never lusted for the color of trout
in a pool a mile away.

He knew from the smoke in the sky
Mrs. Johnson was starting supper, and, in March,

when the candles appeared,
he knew Bobby's boy had died.

My ghost only ever had one bar
where the keeper didn't water his drinks,

nor did he feel the need to hide his moth cap,
his potato clothes, or scrub himself birth pink.

My ghost tells me there was a time you'd look out
and not find a Dairy Queen. You could sit

on your porch a whole life and never think
about China. Sometimes I see my ghost

bringing cut sunflowers to his wife
and it seems so simple.

Then, sometimes, it is dark,
he's just in from work and Griswold says

they ain't going to raise his pay. And even back then
the power went out, long nights when they had no kerosene.

And my ghost tries to sell me on simpler times:
the grass soft, endless —

lampless nights,
pools of crickets singing.

Thirteen

The trees outside my window are dense.
Out there a man could lose his self;
grow his hair, brother the deer. The trees
know the past will be present again;
if not in the bark, then in the mulch.

When we were boys we could hear so well
the waves sanding the cliff. But we could not
see the edge. The four of us running
and cutting in the crowded dusk towards
the push of gravity. One night I got lost
and the wet branches fingered my face.
I'd never had a woman but when I did,
I'd remember how the earth was a velvet suck.
I took off my shirt, wrapped it tourniquet tight
round a stick and—with my brother's zippo
—lit it up.

I can still see my flame out there;
my hair shank long, fingers sharp.

Cassella : The Pastor's Son

The team did not like Cassella's methods but
Jesus, he could run. Made it look like floating.
He was born to it: his calves like loaves, thighs
thick sides of beef. First, we'd run the lake loop,
then attack the steep hills. He'd take us on the rise,
our captain patting our shoulders, our butts.
After the runs, legs stammering, arms scratched,
we'd find him waiting in his father's van.
The fastest could sit up front, choose the tape.

> When his name made the news mom kissed her cross
> said, *Jesus. He was always such a good boy.*

He kept his stash in the glove box, let us boys
draw and glow in back, legs burnt from the run.
We'd drive to his house, listen to The Dead.
Cassella said this was our time to commune,
pray, talk sport, speak our blessings, repent
before the "cool down" in his dad's basement.
We are a team, he'd say, then have us close our eyes,
let him gently clean our spirits, maybe our souls.
In the way that his father taught him, they said.

> On Sunday Mom doubled her donation,
> dyed her hair red in the sink. *Jesus,*
> the pastor said, offered St. Sebastian's prayer.

Hunter Boy & Girls at the Stream

The boy watches from the muscled hill.
All around is green but the water cuts dark.
The girls are deer grazing, smoking long cigarettes.
They have not shaved for him, the hills, the water.
On their mouths is the taste of mint, he is sure
the cigarettes have been stolen from Mother.
He recognizes the gold glint of the brand.
His sister's friend removes her plain tank-top.
The deer, unfazed, watch his sister follow.
Hers are bigger, smooth as heavy rocks found
at the bottom of the stream where he tickles trout.
They are fresh, white nets — pink tips of good bait.

He feels the current, the rising of water.
His sister rests on her elbows, touches
a hard spine. And then comes the shower:
the boy, stones stocked at his feet. His sister,
her friend; blushing red targets.

I Was a Fat Boy

I was so hungry then and the world
held every candy I could imagine. Now,
I cannot imagine what it would be like to ride
up the hills I knew when I was fat. When stars
were still milk dazzlers and the moon was cheese
above the trees, I'd talk myself to sleep. Now,
I'm on a train for Paris. I am the line
on the horizon as today turns into tonight—

I am an empty house,
my face is nameless. A thin man catches
my eye from a garden. I've not felt
so hungry for a while. The world is not mine,
my heart wobbles like yolk.

Tomorrow the Red Birds

will eat the dead mosquitoes.
I could ask him what poison
there was in his air, what he ate
and drank as a boy that made him.
Do I call, listen
to his silence,
the soft chug
of his breath?
Do I call, say, "this
is your son and I've been thinking
of cancer 'cause the orange men
are coming to spray the trees"?
Or do I just
fasten the windows,
caulk the cracks, pull
the picnic table inside,
hope nothing gets in.

Everybody Always Talking About Jesus

I got a girl up the attic
the summer I turned ten. Her shirt went damp
and we played a game where I'd strip and she'd slap

my calves with my dead grandma's cane.
One afternoon she took my clothes
and left me up with the heat and dust, mothballs

fermenting like apples. I was nailed in.
She had lunch or baked bread, played nurse with her dolls
or something. I could hear my mother,

her vacuum scowl. I saw the sunlight snatch the shadows,
heard my father slam the door. After the third hour the girl rose
with my clothes and a switch from her yard.

I was so happy, I took it all; her arms sweating
like horses. My father and sister never knew
but in that house noise always dried like palm.

After Dad's funeral everybody was talking about Jesus
and how we should listen to what he said.

II

Sis and I purge his boxes of books,
finding a faded Polaroid of a red-head
that was not my mother:

Garters cling to her thighs and her ass
is wide and rosy as if slapped
or left out in the December snow.

I guess I always knew my dad was not
a pious man. It's sick, my sister says,
but my eyes stay on the woman,

recognizing her from the back row
of graduation and high school plays.
My sister sticks the photo between parched papers

and I think about dozens of times I saw the make
of dad's car parked down side roads but never checked
the plates. I was the good boy. The one he wanted.

III

I'm still up in the attic, going red with the girl,
the color of my hair lapsing. And I feel so naked
in Dad's house with my sister, I walk around modest

like my balls are tucked into a loincloth. And, at night,
in the old house—the house he willed to her—
I keep thinking about Jesus, about all the talk

and how they all say to obey. We don't know
if he was an alcoholic or kept a mistress. We don't know
how badly he wanted to be on that cross. But the house,

I keep thinking, I could use that scratch. These days
Rosie wants pregnant so bad I barely touch her. So,
before Sis goes to bed I tell her, we can split everything—

Dad left me the car, you can have half the car. But no,
she says, the car's seen too many stations
she doesn't want to think about. She spits

her toothpaste and I watch
the light beneath her door
till it's gone.

Night Nurse

It's the last of her six night shifts.
He'll have left for the field
by the time she gets home.

And the copper man
has been dying for days,
disappearing into his sheets.

His son only visited once.
The tests will always be positive.
He'll never leave her, it's his blood.

She takes her breaks in his doorway,
knows he will be gone by morning.

Under Hotel Sheets

And the mother with scarlet baby biting
her breast, and the trucker with the bullet whore, crying

though he'd like to do more. And the newlyweds
too poor to go too far – but still he brings crimson,

and the nurse escapes, blots her mascara
on paper sheets which dry an ink spill,

and the farmer sweats the night
and goes back to grass the next day,

and the male too scared to shit,
waits for the balloons to break.

And only yesterday I was told
of my grandmother below hospice sheets,

and there's angel dust in skeletal lamp light,
brown, moth-size burns left on the shade.

And someone looked out this window,
and someone spilled wine for the floor

and you have to tell yourself without fear
where this goes, and what we leave,

what remains whenever
we are a little bit gone. And how many

others have had this bed and done
what I've done — come in a hand

beneath whispering sheets,
wiped their ghosts on white before sleep?

The Grave-tender

Weekly my hands work in her dirt.
The soil, sometimes fertile, says *gravity takes all.*
I remember her skin sagging like a lost kite,
her head wrinkled, dangling thin from her body.

The soil, sometimes fertile, says *gravity takes all.*
I prune the tulips in winter:
heads wrinkled, dangling thin from the stems.
I edge around her stone. Finger her soil, turn it.

I've pruned the tulips in winter,
swept the snow from her polished head; my hands,
edging around her stone, fingered her soil, turned it
soft as cotton, begging the growth of spring.

I've swept the snow from her young head
with a mitten or the end of my scarf,
softest cotton; begging the push of spring.
Like her body, once mine, now gone to seed.

With a mitten or the end of my scarf
I'd tap her blushed face, play her like a kitten.
Her body (like mine, now going to seed)
frays and rots despite this quiet tending.

The Water is Cold

and my grandfather is dying.
I'm calf deep in it, my knees
tickled by violet waves.
I ask the salted woman,

"How many swimmers today?"
She says *none*,
sucks her orange teeth, lies.
None of the grey ones went in.

But her kid, I saw him; his supple ribs,
flat nipples, and royal blue veins
splashed into the sea. I was Aschenbach
watching her beautiful boy.

I followed him.
Let my lungs go numb, lay
in the green murk,
adrift in the spectrum.

Gasoline

A week ago I spilled
a can of gasoline onto the dirt
floor of the barn.

A full gallon soaked into the earth.
Since then, I've had headaches,
can't catch my balance.

And I can still smell the gas
from twenty yards away.
It reminds me of hitching west

and this ride I hooked
in the back of a truck
the color of rust.

When I shook the driver's hand
he smiled, his teeth like a caterpillar,
and I knew I was beat.

The guy kept all these rags back there,
soaked in gasoline. It was warm
and I fell asleep cocooned in reek.

When I came to, it was almost time
to get out. I could feel caterpillars on me,
thought I was going to suffocate.

> He said the free ride was over, it was
> only a matter of time, and I didn't wish to be
> out west, didn't care to sit

in any more cars with strangers and talk
about the pace or weather back east.

I tried to lose the smell in a stream,
thought I sent it upriver, away
like father, the attic, his ties.

They Will Go On

The western horizon is still lightning blue.
To the east, everything is side-of-the-bridge grey.
I am patient as trees and flowers, desert cacti.

The grandkids hide inside with swollen eyes
and I want the rain to come quick, slap
their pale necks. I've counted the summers left

and the young should take this rain beside me
as I took father's wheat, corn, and whole bloody harvest.
I roll one more September cigarette,

Summer coughs her last cough;
a dribble from which the children hide,
stay dry as rain loosens soil.

Oregon Trail

October, still
the west is open.

Tonight sleep. Tomorrow
wake and still the west.

We'll send colors:
postcards of nothing,

of range and empty pink.
Postcards of more west.

Wake and still October,
the west open. Pink.

The Apartment

Our new walls,
empty in the dusk,
hang like sheets
before first light.

There is a driven nail
by the stove that could
hold a pan if the walls
stay sturdy. And the

                    old tenants left a mirror in the
                    bedroom which looks back at
                    staring walls with fine cracks
                    like a museum's basement vase.

                    There are brown smears
                    in the study; chocolate, blood
                    or shit, we don't know what
                    will happen to us here or what

will settle on rented walls
or if nothing will settle
at all. We've just moved

                    and already we are bitter
                    cranberries in each other's
                    mouths, biting about photos,
                    the place of the table, lay

of the bed. The apartment is a City
Hall we cannot fight. So we turn
like lawyers, against each other,
let the walls stare. There is a mirror

          to look into, a nail to hang onto.
          Our unopened boxes hide in corners
          and closets like beaten children.
          And we will take the blood

off the walls and the dust
from the shelves. We have one
year together in a place that
is empty at dusk and feels like fog

          inside and between us,
          and Christ, tomorrow
          we will live here.

The First Time I Touched Her

At the party, we sit, taste fish
with our tongues, our noses.

My wife is a purple scent
the whole table can see.

Hard scales still on my hands
from the work when I was poor.

Never am I a man
who hasn't tinned, deboned.

Sometimes I rough
perfume into my palms. And they sit,

eat the swollen fish,
spit the delicate bones

to the side. After coffee my eyes rest
on the lawn. Sandalwood lingers in the air.

I say little, sheath my right
hand deep in my pocket,

remember the hard work, her face
in the bathroom mirror, her teeth

almost laughing. The heat off her
slippery neck as she tried

to scream and the smell,
that first time, of sweet pot-pourri.

Our Door, After a Turbulence

I am always depressed
        after hard turbulence,
        the craft shaking like paper

finding myself alive
        and not at my funeral
        with no one looking
        for my little bones,
        my diaries of marrow.

See, I loved you always
        and always I dream
        that you will look for me,
        find a sign in my bones,
        craft a sternum pendant.

And I am surprised
        as them when we land
        and our world continues
        with a stamp and a taxi
        till I am at our door,
        sucking my breath
        before turning the key.

Knots

She is a god of knots.
His socks are Spanish Bows
and in the night the doors
are secured with a tight Sheep Shank,

china cups hang on Artillery Loops
and she twists her own hair
when she worries, pulls it
over and around and then through

and around again until it hangs
in a Jury Mast and some nights,
when the door is tight, she gets him
in a Carrick Bend and whispers

about the old Bill Hitch
and all the time he hopes
she's tied herself up
enough to stay the storm.

Stain

Dusk, and Martha's been waiting all day.
Her laundry wants down from the line.

She's tied half the bottle watching
clouds grow, "Gonna storm," she says.

The dog wags its tail by the door.
Fall is coming down and soon

she'll just dump our clothes
in the dryer and be done.

She sends me out.
I taste the empty air,

the dog breaks for the trees.
Our shirts and socks are stiff,

I fold them like stale dough.
Inside, her TV turns on and I shake

Martha's linen shirt, find the stain—
burgundy cooled to a limp pink—

and I want to take this
to the bath, scrub it

with nail and wire brush,
open the drain and let the color away.

Babel

Our good sex was building
a Babel. We were fucking
our way up the tower
and God saw us coming.
And so there came
months we could not
fuck. We remembered
the tower as it was written:
The people God slung
all over the Earth, speaking
incoherent to each other
as we do when you moan
the dishes, say I don't listen.
And when I say you cut
the bread crooked or
over-salt the pasta you hear
my words as Greek and I know
our sex was looked at
and the Lord said: "Look,
they are one people
and they have all one
language; and this is only
the beginning of what
they may do." And so
you come to me at night,
and some nights I come
before you: humble flesh,
with a different tongue.

The Slip (pt. 2)

And driving today,
after all that stuttering time,
your hand was scratching
at the faint slug of a scar.

A long time ago,
reaching for a banana,
I fell off a stool,
cutting my knee. You,

because we were good then,
didn't spit, just cleaned it,
dressed it, made it okay.

And driving today, you found it again.
But the weather was too poor for us. Rain
fell like diamonds. We could not afford.

to change direction,
drive to the dead end
where we used to go
when we were drunk

and just wanted to move.
We passed that turnoff
like it was never there,
your moist hand awakening my knee.

Bluegrass

The day is pink meat and almost done.
I take a drink. Maggie boils our corn.
I look to the mowed lawn, know the clippings
feed our garden then turn straw pale by June.
I get red-lipped, cosy as a camp-fire,
remembering: I held the phone for him.

And this was long ago, a decade or more.
For once the whole house kept mind of itself.
All of us, even Tuna Dave, stayed quiet.
I held my breath by the sex of his strings.
He plucked falsetto through *Red Dirt Girl*,
his banjo shivering like skin at each caress.

One note was a leather whip in a field
of daisies, the next an autumn leaf.
The National Radio Man listened
from New York City and said, Boy
you've got to get north. We'll pay the whole fare,
Just come. And that was it.

The house broke up. No more camp fires
or late nights with our instruments. The smell
of good grass left the air. Some of us still
stay in touch but we don't know where he is,
if he made it up to New York or quit
in Nashville or went, like Tuna,

into the cans and bottles. It was long ago;
the music was rich as the tanneries,
like the grass used to be down here.
But it is something more I miss
when Maggie shouts my name,
says the corn is ready now.

The Day He Went to War

was bright, white and clean; an advertisement
for fresh laundry, lady things, or whatever.

we watched him from joe's garage, our music clanging;
hub caps and tin cans thrown against cement.

we watched his mother watch the car
that took him, saw her wave at nothing,

then, we took it from the top:
one, two, a—one two three four

Retrieving the Dead

The losing army litters the roads we've paved.
We ride on the dead, getting to town, going home.
The dark raccoon, a sun-blind dog at midday.
We slow, drive in low gear till the guilt's blown.
Rain and maggots take the flesh. But,
sometimes the stench sticks in our entrails.
We have our own stones, the smell ruins a veal cut;
a neighbor calls the town council
and I come in jeans with a shovel and an orange truck.
All summer the roads tally bodies like bumps
of fur and blood from route 11 to Walnut.
I peel the carnage, haul the dead to the dump,
lift the soldiers up, try not to breathe till they're tossed
into our trenches of tea bags, messed diapers, spare parts.

Necessary Astronomy

We had one of those
conversations like necessary
astronomy which your mind
must get back to
again and again to tell you something
about who you are and how you can exist.
In your mind
maybe you are Paul Newman eating eggs,
maybe you are Orion tightening his belt,
maybe we are,
all of us, still 23 and drinking
as if we were stars who could drink
and not burn
out what was between us.
And it is important that we never fuck;
not on that night
or ever and after, anyway, we
lost touch, but that night was something
that I come back to
like a constellation an uncle showed me
and if you die
before me, Erin, I will not go to your funeral
and try to make
my mouth give everyone that image of you
in December,
our heads touching, your cuts
like all the skies we loved, opening
and closing and opening
again, echoes of necessary people chatting,

organizing lights
inside a darkness that grows and disperses
in the sky outside.

The Flood

Furniture, photos,
petals floating in water.

It was spring and the river
bloomed and rose.

They Tore The Bridge Down a Year Later

I

I found her in a blue dress
beneath the old wooden bridge
with ropes round her wrists,
her neck, her ankles.

It's how we would tie a hog,
when there was money
for that type of thing.

Her hair was perfect
but, by the time Powell got her to Texas,
her dress looked like it had caught
the wrong side of a horse.

A year later the new bridge goes up.
All clean cable and wire,
so the cars can drive too fast
and my boy and I can't sit there,
let the water pass.

As a kid, I'd rest on the splintered rail, protected
in the strong shade of the cyprus pines,
drop pennies or spit onto the frogs of Cow Creek
back when the water ran clear.

But they said a good car couldn't cross it.
So I guess the children
who used to throw pennies, spit,
had to find something new.

I still see the old bridge,
pennies rusting in water.

I remember they told me
Falyssa Van Winkle was ten
and she got raised
a little north of here.

They said she went to buy peanuts
at some flea market in Beaumont
and her mother watched Falyssa go,
kept hawking clay ashtrays
and heavy magnifying glasses;
nothing fancy, just stuff
people sometimes need.

Five hours later Falyssa
was under the bridge I used to spit off
and Powell was cleaning his mobile home,
readying to drive north.

Nowadays I don't pass the creek much.
There is no reason to walk my quiet boy
across metal into Louisiana.

If the bridge I knew still stood
maybe I could bring him down,
tell him the lawn can wait. Tell him

his father wants to pass the time,
make him talk.
But the bridge is not there anymore.

Somebody told me Powell made it
into the papers, said his last words
were, "I am ready for my blessing."

And Falyssa's bag of salted peanuts
has run down, met the big river.
That last thing of hers, heading for the ocean.

Ode for a Rain from Death Row

The rain is a cold, clean prayer,
the only light I want to see.
I say it still rains on her

like it rains on the bars and streets
somewhere outside the walls.
And in the rain, she is always twenty,

her shoes always candy-red Converse,
her jeans always damped to her thighs,
her mouth never parted from mine.

She hasn't pressed her lips to glass
since the fire; the ashes are back to ashes, the dust
follows dust, the spring rain powders her arms

and evaporates in the stare of the sun.
And this rain is the only light I want to see.
A mist that kisses till my socks are sponge,

till the fire fizzles and baby is back again
cooing with hot-chocolate-warm hands.
Before I die I want to stand outside,

birth-naked, let the Lord soak me.
But options and pardons are gone.
The priest only offers a glass

where my throat wants a holy rain that pours
in sheets and hoods and lasts for forty days,
till it floods, and floats my sins away.

I Got Out When It All Went Down

I'm no longer dead in the morning
fetal and afraid to start the day.
I don't get stuck in the subway
or scan the shadows of streets.
This life is better than Betty
and all that was, but lately, the lights
flicker whenever I walk past.
I don't know, maybe it's just
the hard labor, but I feel the dark
and nobody in Nicetown knows
about dust. It's starting to itch me,
what I did, and maybe Pennsylvania
isn't far enough. Maybe there is a place
you can pull peaches and oranges
from trees. I wake from dreams
thinking, *I am not a soul.*
Then, last night, in the bar,
they were all watching
Fox News again. Nobody looked
at me. And I wanted to say,

> it was best, what happened. I never
> liked those buildings: their shadows
> froze everything. Mornings, walking
> into their long trench coats, was like
> walking into slabs of ice. And once
> I saw Betty where I did not expect
> to see her: hailing a cab way the fuck
> down on 15th and I thought, *Christ,*
> I was not where I should have been
> that morning, started for work a little late.
> Ditched my phone near the chaos, crashed

at the Port Authority. And it is a small comfort
that my photo hung on the walls
with the murdered, that maybe
she'll have enough money now.
I like to picture her going to that hole,
the sun on her face and a new man
on her arm. Safe, thinking my bones
are buried, that the past is the past
is the past, and I am not coming home.

Open the Connections, She Says.

Cords of wood, lines of concrete, aluminum
slats covering new houses. Mortar
crossing pavement and cobblestone, endless
bricks raising, connections of lawn and mansion.
Her face
         was a new skyscraper; Chicago
at night. Sunglasses on the dancefloor.
Now she throws food on the ground for a cat.
The cat finds a dog and gums his tail.
She opens
         doors all over the house,
opens windows and the house breathes
like the soil connected to the crop.
She says, let the dust dance
in the shotgun
         beams. Her chair, her needle, wool,
she says, are only objects now. Her garden
inhales damp air at night, exhales
the day. Watch the shore, she says,
the ocean
         is a lung. Watch the garden
from the atmosphere of the roof. She used
to sit in the club wearing sunglasses, watching
the cats connect with dogs. She used to rock
on her chair connecting wool to wool.
But then

she had to open her house,
connect it to the dry air, the soil.
Had to bury her dog to help flowers grow.
Sometimes
she watches his crucifix and tries
to see God where wood connects to wood.

Last Night, I Should Have Driven Straight Home

Today the breakers are clear,
sharp, sure in the sun.

And out there, in the squint of distance,
the waves have conversations.

They do not stop.

Somewhere out there in all the talk talk talk,
somewhere out there sits Paris, all the lights.

The waves hit the rocks hard for a secret.

And I believe the clouds will burn,
leave the day to blue sky,

sweating white sand, screens of heat
obscuring everything.

The seaweed yawns ashore.

Somewhere the Sacre Coeur and closer:
a kitchen, beans soaking, an apron

tied tight around a growing waist.

Waiting for the Ocean

Cover myself in blankets
of dust. Cover myself

in a second-hand poncho
Virginia Woolf could have worn

with her pockets turned inside out,
the light tongues of fabric licking

at the salted California sun.
It can take some time

and she keeps saying
she was drawn to me.

There is an attic of time
which I hide in, time

where we walk blank beaches
that never get cold,

visit bright houses which cast no shadows
onto pink shores. We pause on the coast,

her hands freckle and brown
and her hair lightens a little.

People say to her—*You
look good.* And I say—

The chairs were flying.
They aimed for my head.

And I say, *I was drawn to you*
by the chairs and she understands

and never calls the weather mundane
or melodramatic. And the ocean stays

in front and below:
unknown and living with us.

Also, it is Lambing Season

Call the flowers yellow. Nearby, nothing is wrong:
children pull at their mother's hems outside church,

lambs saturate a field, working their mother's tit, testing
strength on the soft ground I tread. And if their eyes

are old enough perhaps they see a shadow, a figure of black,
crossing from the gate towards the stream. And if their hearts

have instinct perhaps they tremble as their mothers take the tit
and hurry, in one mind, flanking my left and right, hooves gutting

the muck. They bare their yellow teeth, hurl scrappy grunts
that burr like Dad's Chrysler before it died, like bagpipes beaten

with sheet metal, like God herself crying, away, get away from these,
my babies, mine. The mothers surround and, for a spell, the lambs

are lost behind, tripping to stand. With my right hand I open,
then close, the fence and look back into a row of black stares

        and the lambs, ignorant of what my trespass was,
        return to sucking sweet from their mothers, living

        at the breast pulling milk by the neck-full.
        And I wanted to put my hands and knees

into the mud, wanted to sponge dirt into my jeans,
my jumper, be a lamb again. Easter was coming.

I was not in the country of my birth. Shadows
were all around me. My mother's milk was sepia.

Unfinished Rooms

YELLOW ROOM

For two years
it was a bare light bulb
by the side of the bed.

It was Tom Waits
if Tom Waits
was a light bulb.

I never found a shade that fit
and in summer I'd watch moths
swing low, singe their wings.

It was an attic room
with a slanted ceiling
and there were times

when it was so still,
cold and quiet,
it felt like camping.

BROWN ROOM

There was one room where I was on top
and she was drunk, but competent
with her hand, her skin

    and my mouth was cotton dry, then wet
    and on the floor with us
    were stacks of parched books,
    books with thin, petite fonts.
    Like the back of a library, this room.

And it was only luck which stopped us,
let us finish with our others, in other
more furnished, less closeted quarters.

RED ROOM

After painting the room brothel red,
smears of paint stuck
to the curve of her breast.

Late at night, we smelled the paint dry.
She had red dawning on her thigh.

This was something ripe I took, didn't mind
                              the smell.
By morning I was nauseous, my head stained
                              by deep oil.

She wanted to hang her pictures on dry,
scarlet walls: a neat row of postcards,
the Japanese print over the fireplace.

And I wanted to go for a long walk,
shake my hair in the wind.
Never know what she chose.

GREEN ROOM

She kept a Christmas tree
in the corner for four months.
By the time I pulled her
it was all branches.
The needles stuck
to our bare feet
and we brought them to bed,
furnished each other.
In the morning
her curtains
played shadows
on open walls.
She'd meant to hang
fairy lights and tapestries
but then the tree died,
the lease was up and
the carpet was covered
in pines.

WHITE ROOM

My parents pulled
everything out:

the comics
from the closet

the LPs
the cassettes

the posters
the paperbacks.

The stains scrubbed
from the cream carpet.

The mattress my virginity sunk into
sits at the Salvation Army.

Home is not
a recognized place.

Home is a room
with a mirror

leaning against
the wall.

No thumbtack holes,
no coffee rings

on the nightstand.
A halogen light,

clean, surgical sheets.
It is almost done,

they say,
just a few more things

and the room
will be complete.

And Table, You are Made of Wood

If you could drink the white wine that sucks
      your color the way jellyfish pull shade from sand
would you get drunk and speak loudly
      of worthless sacrifice, the rings you lost,
and show those not listening
      your secret thumb, pennies of war?
Would you invite the devil to dance on you
      and unleash blazing urine on the dull?
I could be you, dear table,
      so much wine and rings and we could speak
of scratches—

      of lost energy and solid waiting.
I too have been cut, had my meaning moved
      far from where I thought it was.

NOTES

MY 100-YEAR-OLD GHOST: This poem is indebted to Bill McKibben's book, *The Age of Missing Information* (Random House, 1992).

THEY TORE THE BRIDGE DOWN A YEAR LATER: The murder of Falyssa Van Winkle in October 1990 was mentioned in Dina Temple-Raston's *A Death in Texas* (Holt Paperbacks, 2003).

RETRIEVING THE DEAD: This poem is indebted to Barry Lopez's book, *About This Life: Journeys on the Threshold of Memory* (Harvill Press, 1999) and in particular his essay on road kill, "Apologia."

ODE FOR A RAIN FROM DEATH ROW: This poem is indebted to Kenny Ritchie's quote in *The Manchester Observer* on January 21, 2006. He said, "My dearest wish before I die is to stand outside in Scottish rain and to feel it soak me."

Lightning Source UK Ltd.
Milton Keynes UK
UKOW03f1922301013

220116UK00008B/179/P